Why Saving Can Send You Broke

Money Habits That Keep You From Having More

Stephen Outram & Simone Phillips

ISBN: 978-0-9943327-9-0

Date Published: 1 August 2025

For everyone who thought they were wrong with money, and were never wrong at all

"Choice creates.
What are you choosing?"
—Gary Douglas

Acknowledgements

T his book would not exist without the people who have generously contributed to our awareness, choices, and to our lives.

To Gary Douglas, thank you for being willing to look at what so many people would rather ignore, and for never telling us what to think, only inviting us to know.

To Dr. Dain Heer, thank you for showing us how ease and joy can change everything, including the energy we have with money.

And finally, to you, the reader, thank you for picking up this book, playing with the questions, seeing what you haven't seen before, and choosing a greater life. Nothing makes this book more alive than you choosing more.

Contents

Prologue

S imone and I didn't write this book because we were confused about money.

We wrote knowing something different was possible.

I've lived a life. I've made money, spent money, had none, and had plenty. I've run businesses. I've asked questions. I've educated myself. I enjoy money, and I enjoy awareness even more.

And over time, I started to see that so much of what people believe about money ... doesn't actually work.

Not because they're wrong, but because the world they're trying to fit themselves into is too small for who they really are.

This book isn't a fix.
It's not a system or a plan.
It's a conversation, one you get to have with yourself as you read.

You'll find questions, stories, observations, and a few gentle challenges. If something in these pages makes you lighter, freer, more curious, follow that. It may just be your awareness knocking.

Thanks for being here. You don't have to agree with anything in this book. You don't even have to like it.

But if it invites you to see something you couldn't see before, that might be the beginning of everything.

—Simone and Stephen

Introduction

M any books about money tell you how to get more of it.

They offer a system, a strategy, a plan. Save this. Spend that. Budget here. Invest there.
Follow the steps, reach the goal, and maybe, if you do it all just right, you will have more money in the end.

There is nothing wrong with that. More money is wonderful.

But what if the money isn't the whole story?
What if the real limit isn't how much you earn, but what you are willing to have?

What if you could see the hidden points of view shaping every choice you make with money, and choose something greater?

That is what this book invites you to do.

Money is Part of Life, Not the Point of It

Money is important. It buys things, opens doors, creates comfort and choice. But money is not the source of your freedom — *you are.*

Everything in this book is about you:

The choices you make.
The targets you set.
The stories you keep alive about spending, saving, debt, and wealth.
The ceilings you did not know you had.
The structures you inherited from people who lived in a world very different from yours.

Nothing is Wrong. Nothing Needs Fixing.

Let's be clear: you are not broken.
There is no problem here, only choices you have made, and new choices you can make now if you would like to.

You do not have to destroy your budget or run away to Bali to "find yourself." You do not have to rebel against your parents, your teachers, your old boss, or the system.

You only need to look at what you believe about money and about the life you are living with it, and ask,
Does this work for me now?
If yes, great. Keep choosing it.
If not, you can choose again.

What You Will Find Here

This book is a conversation.
A conversation with you and, if you would like, with the life you are building.

Inside are stories, reflections, true moments, and questions. Some will be gentle. Some might poke you a little sideways. All are here to help you see what you might be ignoring, not to shame you, but to open the door to something bigger.

Sometimes it is a small shift: the difference between spending money and having it.
Sometimes it is bigger: seeing how you keep debt alive to feel "safe."

Sometimes it is subtle: noticing how much you have already created that you pretend you haven not.

A Quiet Invitation

You do not have to agree with everything here. You do not have to take it all on.

Use what works for you. Leave what does not. Try the questions, if you wish.

And if you find yourself saying, *"I've never thought about money like this before..."* that is more than enough. That small crack of new awareness might be the beginning of everything you did not know was possible.

You are the chooser. You always were.

Let's begin.

Spending vs. Having, Two Different Worlds

It is a curious thing, how so many of us believe we have money, when what we really have is an itch to spend it.

I remember once, early in my career, standing at a furniture store counter, signing the contract for a brand-new bed. It felt solid, adult, like I was "providing for myself" even though, if you had looked at my bank account, you would have found almost nothing there to provide with.

I bought that bed on my first credit card. Slept well on it too, until the credit card bill came. And then for three years, I was still paying for that sleep. Three years of quietly giving away my income every month to own something I had convinced myself I needed now.

Did I "have" money? Not really.

I had a bed.
I had a debt.
And I had a lesson that stayed with me far longer than the bed did.

Spending Money is Easy, Having Money is a Choice

Most people know how to spend. That part is natural, almost a sport. Earning comes next and that can take some training, but it is encouraged. Having is the one nobody really teaches.

If you think about it, most of what we are taught about money is a loop:

- Work to earn → spend → work more to earn → spend again.
  It feels productive. It keeps the economy buzzing. But does it make you wealthy? Not necessarily.

Because having money is different. Having money is not about hoarding. It is not about cutting your life down to fit inside a budget so tight you can't breathe.

It is about choosing to keep some of what flows in, not for a rainy day, not to spend later, but simply to have.

Saving: Spending in Disguise?

I once asked a friend, "Why are you saving?" He looked at me blankly. "To buy a car," he said. "Ah," I said, "so you're not saving to have money, you're saving to spend it."

Most of us do this. We "save" for holidays, for houses, for big things we can not buy all at once. And that is fine, it is part of life. But it is not the same as building wealth.

True wealth starts when you choose to have money, not as an emergency stash, but as a statement to yourself: I can have money and not spend it.

That tiny shift is enormous. It tells the world (and you) that you are not a perpetual spender. You are someone who can keep.

How to Have Money: The 10% Account

Here is something practical, if you would like to try it.

When money comes in, take 10% of it and set it aside. Not for bills. Not for holidays. Not for the new whipper snipper on Marketplace. Just to have.

You will be amazed at how quickly this changes you. Not just your balance, you. You start to see yourself as someone who has money. Even if it is only a small amount at first, the act of having teaches you something that budgeting alone never will:

You do not need to spend everything to prove you have it.

What Does Your Life Cost?

Now, I am not saying throw out your budget. Budgeting is a tool, it can be wise, freeing, even a relief. But too many people use budgeting as a cage.

Knowing exactly what your life costs to run gives you awareness, not limitation. It shows you whether you are creating a life you can afford, or a life that demands more than you are willing to have.

When you know the real numbers, the coffees, the subscriptions, the insurance, the impulse buys, you stand on solid ground. From there, you can ask: Would I like to shrink my life to fit this number? Or: Would I like to create more money so this number doesn't matter so much?

The difference is everything.

Questions to Carry Forward

Here are some questions to play with:

- Are you someone who only knows how to spend?
- Are you willing to practice having?

What might your life look like if having money was just as easy, just as natural, as spending it?

Take a breath. Look at your next paycheck, sale, invoice, or surprise windfall. Take your 10%. Smile at it. Leave it there. Let it sit like a quiet promise that you too, can have.

An easy way to do this is set up an extra account with your bank and deposit your ten percents there.

Up Next

Next, we'll look at a kind of spending that doesn't even feel like spending, borrowing. You may think you're buying freedom. But what if you're actually committing your future to lack?

What if having money isn't about earning more, but about receiving more than you've allowed before?

Are You Indebted to Your Future?

M ost people think debt is about money. It isn't, really. It is about trust.

More precisely, it is about a lack of trust in your ability to have money now, so you borrow from your future self to pay for today's life.

A swipe of the card here. A tap there. "I'll pay for it later." The contract slides across the counter. The thing you desire is yours, but the price? That has become a visitor in your future.

The strange thing is: because the debt is "not here yet," most people treat it like it is not real. They pay-off the minimum each month. They resent the bill, blame the lender, and joke about "bad luck" or "living paycheck to paycheck." However, beneath that is a choice they made, and keep making: to stay indebted to their future.

Debt as Forced Discipline

A friend of mine was just $8,000 away from paying off her home loan. She could taste freedom, the house would be hers, outright. The debt could be gone with a single payment.

But when we talked about it, she told me something that made my mind boggle: she was scared.

She said, *"If I pay it off, I don't trust myself to save. I know I'll just spend the money. The debt keeps me disciplined."*

So instead of clearing it, she bought a few expensive items. $20,000 here, $40,000 there. And rolled them into the home loan. Just like that, the debt was "safe" again. Now it was unpayable in one hit. And she was "safe," too, safe from her own freedom.

This is not unusual. Many people secretly treat debt like forced savings. They do not trust themselves to keep money, so they hand that power to the bank.

The trouble is, this is the exact opposite of having money. The bank always wins. The future gets weighed down. And real wealth stays just out of reach.

The Hidden Cost of Debt

Debt means you are spending money you do not have yet. It means your future, which should be yours to create as you wish, is already claimed by past choices.

When you carry debt, you are carrying yesterday forward. Every payment keeps it alive. Every resentful minimum payment keeps it alive. The debt becomes like an old relationship you cannot quite break up with.

You may even notice: the bigger your debt, the more you find ways to not look at it. The future can not be felt yet, so it's easy to pretend it's not there. But here is the truth: the future arrives, moment by moment, whether you want it to or not. Sooner or later, you will be forced to look.

How to Stop Choosing a Future of Debt

If you want to break the cycle, you have to do something unusual, **get present with your debt.**

Be more present with it than the bank is.

Here is how:

1. Make it real.

Write it all down. Every line of credit, every loan, every dollar owed. Do not hide it in an app you never open. See it in black and white. Know it. There is power in putting pen to paper.

2. Make a plan.

Do not just hope it will "go away." Choose how you will pay it down. Maybe you pay a little more each week. Maybe you sell something that is weighing you down more than it frees you up.

3. Commit.

If you have to live with less spending money for a while, so be it. The freedom you gain is worth far more than the thing you would buy next.

4. Stop feeding it.

Debt likes to sneak back in. Watch the moments you want to borrow from your future again. Ask, *Do I need to create more money instead? Or: Can I choose not to buy this, just for now?*

The Other Side of Debt

Some debts are practical:

A home loan,

an investment,

a tool for business growth.

There is nothing "wrong" with debt itself. The question is: *Is your debt serving you, or are you serving it?*

There is a big difference between using debt as a tool and using debt as a way to control yourself because you do not trust your choices.

When you pay debt down, you reclaim that trust. You show yourself: I can have money. I can be free. I do not need to tie up my future to discipline myself today.

A Small Story About Receiving

This reminds me of another woman I knew, my own mother. She spent much of her life in debt. She was never really willing to receive money. When a windfall came through marriage later in life, she found herself with a widow's pension when her husband passed away.

25

We spent hours trying to convince her to keep the pension. She wanted to give it away, all of it, to charity. She had spent so many years refusing to receive that when money finally arrived at her door, she couldn't stand to let it stay.

It took a lot of persuasion and some yelling too, to get her to keep it.

So this chapter is not just about paying down debt. It is about something bigger: Are you willing to receive money? *Are you willing to have it, without needing to spend it or pushing it away?*

A Question for You

Look at your debt, big or small, old or new.
Ask yourself: What future am I really creating with this?

Is it freedom? Or a long, slow promise to keep paying yesterday's choices forward?

And if you would like freedom, it starts here, in this moment, with this simple choice: *Stop stealing from your future. Start trusting yourself, now.*

Next up

We will look at targets and goals and how many people do not appreciate the difference. This difference has a big impact on your capacity to go again and again, never failing.

What is Your Target?

T here is a difference between having a
goal and having a target.

Most people do not see the difference, they use the
words as if they are interchangeable. But when
looking deeper, the meanings are worlds apart.

A goal is something you "should" reach. An end
point, fixed. Like a finishing line in a race, cross it
and you are done. Or you are not done, and then
you feel like a failure.

A target though, that is alive. A target is something
you aim at, again and again, like pulling back the
string of a bow and letting the arrow fly. Maybe you
miss the first shot. Maybe you miss a hundred. But

you have still got the bow, the arrows, and your hands. You can choose to aim again.

The Etymology of a Limit

I like words. They show us what we really believe, even when we are not aware of it.

Goal comes from the idea of a boundary, an obstacle, a barrier at the end of a race. In Old English, gal meant "to hinder." The word itself carries the sense that once you hit it, you are stopped.

Many people set goals the same way they run a race: flat out, with a single-minded push. But when they reach the finish line, or don't, the energy disappears.

How many people do you know who set a goal to "make a million," and then when they do, they lose it, spend it, or sabotage it? The race ends. They stop creating. They drift until a new "goal" comes along, another limit to chase down.

The Target is Different

A target does not end you, it extends you.

Imagine standing with a bow in your hand. You pick your target, a tree stump, a bale of hay, a bulls eye painted on an old shed wall. You draw back the string. You breathe. You release. The arrow flies.

It lands somewhere. Maybe on target, maybe not. So what do you do? You notch another arrow, adjust your stance, and shoot again. And therein lies the secret, you adjust.

The target has not failed you. You have not failed the target. You are simply in the practice of choosing.

This is how money can work too.

Are You Living for the Goal or the Freedom?

Many people say their goal is "to make money." Fine. But money is not a goal — it is a tool. It is not the finishing line. It is what you use to create something greater.

So what is the real target? Is it freedom? Is it a life that expands each year instead of shrinking? Is it to be the person who knows how to have money and keep having it, no matter what?

If your only target is "make money," you will hit it once and stop. Or you will never hit it at all, because your unconscious point of view keeps shifting the finish line further away.

The target is not just "earn." It is "create." And you can do that again and again, with a thousand arrows if you wish.

When a Goal Becomes a Cage

I have seen people set goals so rigid they cannot breathe inside them.

"I'll pay off the house by 45."
"I'll have a million in the bank by 50."
"I'll retire by 60."

These can be fine milestones, but only if they are flexible. When they become concrete barriers, they trap you. If you miss the date, you judge yourself. If you hit it, you wonder, now what?

The truth is, if you are alive, you are always choosing. The money you earn, the wealth you grow, the ease you allow, they do not stop because you crossed some imaginary line.

What is Your Target Right Now?

Here is something to play with. Grab a piece of paper, or just sit quietly for a moment. Ask yourself:

- What is my target with money?
- Is it a finish line, or an open field I can play in?
- If I miss the target, do I know I can aim again?

And this one:

- If I had no limit on money, what would I create beyond the money itself?

The Practice of Aiming

You will hear people say, *"Set a goal and stick to it."*

I would rather say, *"Choose a target and keep choosing it, again and again."*

Some arrows miss. Some fly further than you imagined. Some hit dead centre. The real freedom is knowing: you are the one holding the bow.

Next up

Let's talk about the choices that really build your future, not the rigid ones that fence you in, but the small, flexible choices that create more than any goal ever could.

Freedom doesn't begin with a number. It begins with knowing you can choose again.

Your Choice Creates

A lot of people think they are waiting for money.

Or waiting for the right moment.
Or the perfect condition.

They say things like:

"I'll buy that car when I get the pay rise."
"I'll book that trip when I save enough."
"I'll get the better bed when I turn 25, or when the kids move out, or when the house is paid off."

They are waiting for the thing, the money, the milestone or the sign, to appear first.

But here is the twist: it is backwards.

The truth is simple. **Choice creates**. Not the other way around.

The Power of Choosing First

When you choose first, you flip the entire flow of your life. The choice is the switch that flicks everything else on.

Choose it, and then the money, the support, the possibilities, the small coincidences and the big surprises, have something to gather around.

I have seen people wait years for "enough money" before they even look at the thing they want. And because they have not chosen it, there is nowhere for the money to land. The possibility never finds a place to grow.

One Caveat, You Have to Allow It

Choosing does not mean demanding. It does not mean forcing a timeline.

When you choose, you also have to allow the universe to play its part, in its own time and shape.

Sometimes what shows up is exactly what you pictured. Sometimes it is far greater.

Sometimes it arrives faster than you imagined. Sometimes it comes sideways, through a person you did not expect, or an opportunity you had not planned.

The Bed or Something Better

I once knew someone who wanted a better bed. They spent months researching mattresses, looking at sales, but never quite chose. They would say, *"I'll get it when I have the spare money."* But the spare money never arrived, because there was no choice, just a wish.

When they finally said, *"Okay, I'm getting a new bed, I don't know how, but I'm choosing it now,"* things shifted. Within a week, they stumbled onto a friend upgrading furniture and got given a luxury bed frame and mattress for next to nothing.

The moment they chose, the universe could conspire. Not before.

Are You Willing to Have It When It Shows Up?

The other piece most people miss is *allowing*.

You cannot choose with one hand and block with the other.

Sometimes the thing you asked for knocks at your door when it is "inconvenient." Sometimes it arrives before you think you are ready.

If you are not willing to receive it when it shows up, you will miss it. The universe did its part, but you did not trust your part.

Try This

Ask yourself:

- What am I waiting for *until*...?
- What would choosing it *now* open up?
- What if I didn't have to know how, *only that I am choosing it?*
- Am I willing to receive it, however it shows up?

Your Future is Made By You

Your life right now is the result of the choices you have made, the ones you know about, and the ones you pretend you did not make.

If you do not like what you see, good news: you can choose again.

Choose bigger. Choose wilder. Choose to create something you can not yet explain.

Money loves movement. Wealth loves courage.

And possibility? It is standing by, waiting for you to choose it first.

Next up

Let's look at how you trust yourself enough to receive it when it comes.

When you choose something, the
Universe begins re-arranging itself.
But only always.

Receiving Money, How Much Can You Really Have?

M ost people say they would like to have more money.

A million would be nice, they say. *Maybe five million, maybe ten.* But the question underneath is more interesting: *Could they really receive it?*

Ka-ching, ka-ching.

Here is where it gets curious. It is one thing to wish for wealth, it is another to allow it to land.

How Much Can You Handle?

Let's play a game.

Imagine you are walking down the street and you see a coin, two dollars, on the footpath. Do you pick it up? Easy. Most people would.

Now imagine you find a wad of notes, a thousand dollars, sitting by a bus stop bench. Do you pick it up? Do you keep it? Or do you look around, certain it is a prank, waiting for someone to jump out with a camera?

Now let's raise the stakes. Same bus stop. Same you. This time, there is a tidy little attaché case. You pop it open and it is stacked with $100,000 in neat bundles.

What do you do?
Pick it up and run? Call the police? Put it back down and pretend you never saw it?

Now let's try ten million. Same suitcase, same bus stop. Could you handle it? Or does your mind immediately fill with crime movies, tax audits, shady characters, mafia chases?

Your Hidden Ceiling

What this game shows is that everyone has a limit, an amount that feels safe to receive. Anything beyond that kicks up all the hidden points of view you did not know you had:

- *If I have too much, people will judge me.*
- *Big money brings big problems.*
- *I wouldn't know how to manage it.*
- *I would have to share it — or hide it.*

So even if you work harder, buy the courses, chase the side hustle, win the lottery, you will unconsciously find ways to drain that money away again.

Are You Letting It In?

Receiving is about more than money. It is about trust. It is about capacity. It is about letting the world surprise you, instead of keeping your life the same small size.

If you can only handle a trickle, you will never allow the flood. Not because the flood is not there, but because you cannot see it without panic.

A Small Exercise

Want to stretch your ceiling?

Close your eyes and picture finding that suitcase with ten million inside. Feel what happens in your gut. What thoughts race through your head? Notice the first excuse your mind jumps to: It's illegal, it's dangerous, it's not mine, I'd mess it up.

Now ask yourself: *Is that true? Or just a story I have learned?*

Try this question: *If I had no point of view about this money, what would I choose?*

Story: The Hidden Ceiling in Real Life

I knew someone who, every time they got ahead, a bit of savings, a pay bump, a surprise bonus, they would somehow find a way to spend it back to zero. They would upgrade the car. The house. A holiday. Something always appeared to absorb the extra.

They did not have a money problem, they had a *receiving limit*. They were comfortable at just-enough, and any more felt like too much to handle.

The ceiling was not out there, it was inside.

Choice Opens, Receiving Allows

Remember: *Choice creates.*

But *receiving* is what lets what you chose show up.

You can choose a million-dollar life, but if your ceiling is stuck at $500, the rest will slip away.

So stretch it. Play with it. Indulge in imagining more than you think you can handle. Be willing to be surprised, and a bit uncomfortable. That is how you know you are growing.

A Question to End

How much more could you receive today, if you did not freak out?

Next up

Let's look at the real cost of your life, and whether you want to shrink it to fit, or expand your revenue to match your bigger targets.

How Much Does Your Life Cost?

H ere is a simple question, *Do you know exactly what your life costs to run?*

Most people do not. Or they sort of do, in rough numbers, half-guessed, rounded up or down, safely vague. They will say, *"Oh, about this much..."* but never really look.

Why? Because seeing the real cost makes it real. And once it is real, you ca not pretend you are not choosing it.

Why Look?

Awareness is not about cutting yourself down. It is about seeing where you stand, so you can choose where you would like to go next.

If you do not know what your life costs, your rent, mortgage, fuel, coffees, subscriptions, impulse splurges, those little "just this once" spends, then you are creating by guesswork.

You are hoping it all works out. Sometimes it does. Often it does not. Either way, you are not choosing consciously, you are drifting.

A Small Story, My Lounge Room Floor

I know what drifting looks like. Around the age of fifty, I was shocked by my own financial situation. My bank account held only $1,000.

I was educated, intelligent, had run my own businesses for thirty years, employed people, appeared successful from the outside,yet there I was: $1,000 to my name. What was going on?

One weekend, I cleared the furniture from my lounge room and made myself a working floor. I laid out every piece of paper I had, bank statements, receipts, income slips, tax records, and started sorting, grouping, adding, tallying.

It took hours. But by the end, I had my real numbers. The truth was simple: I had slowly and steadily been spending more than I earned. A quiet blindness.

It was a Eureka moment. Not comfortable, but freeing. For the first time, I knew what my life cost to run. I could see what I was choosing. And once I knew, I could choose something different.

That moment on the floor changed my life. Fifteen years later, I have freedom, not because I cut everything out, but because I chose awareness first.

Shrink It or Expand It

When you see what your life costs, you get a choice:

- Shrink your life to fit your income or
- Expand your revenue to match the life you would really like to have.

Some people love the simplicity of trimming. They get joy from budgeting down to the cent, living lightly. That is fine, if that is their choice.

Others hate it. They cut the coffees, the treats, the holidays, and end up feeling squeezed. The trouble is, they are cutting life instead of expanding possibility.

There is nothing right or wrong here. Just choice.

Pretending is Expensive

Pretending you do not know costs more than any subscription ever will.

When you do not know what you are spending, you cannot see where you are leaking energy, or money, that could be creating something greater.

Knowing does not mean restricting yourself. It means giving yourself a clear map, so you can choose whether to walk the same path or choose a bigger one.

Try This

Take a piece of paper.
Write down every single thing you spend money on in a month. Every dollar. Every snack, every hidden fee, every automatic charge you "forget."

Do not judge it. Do not cut it yet. Just see it.

Then ask:

Would I like to keep this as it is?

Would I like to shrink it?

Would I like to expand my life and create more revenue instead?

Your Choice, Your Cost, Your Creation

Your life costs something to run. It always will. The question is, Do *you want to live small enough to match your money? Or create enough money to match the life you would love?*

You choose. You always did.

Next up

Let's look at what you already have, including the assets and value you might not be seeing yet.

Many people are saving for a future
they don't even want.

Include All Your Assets

When people think about wealth, they often look in one place.

The money in their account right now. Maybe a few shares. Maybe a bit of superannuation, if they remember to check.

But real wealth is rarely just what is visible. There is so much that stays hidden, sometimes because it is "locked away," sometimes because it is not cash, sometimes because we simply do not acknowledge it.

And when you do not acknowledge what you already have, you cannot choose from the power it gives you. You choose from a smaller story than is true.

Your Invisible Wealth

Take superannuation. Many people forget it is even there until they are close to "retirement age", a phrase that I treat with a grin.

Or inheritance. Some people know they are likely to receive one, but push it out of their mind because it is uncomfortable to think about what makes it possible.

There are other kinds of assets, too: the house you live in, the skills you have built, the people you know, the businesses you have created, the systems that generate money even when you are asleep.

There is the money you could generate by selling something you no longer value, a car, a piece of land, a shed full of tools you never use.

And there is the greatest asset of all: you. The one who chooses, who can create again, and again, and again.

What You Do Not See Can Limit You

If you pretend your wealth is only what you can see in the account today, you might choose fear. Or lack. Or small targets that keep you safe.

When you include the whole picture, you may notice you are wealthier than you thought, not just in dollars, but in possibility.

A Small Story

My partner Simone and I were talking about money, *her* money in particular. She was excited that her 10% account had reached over $100,000 and was now earning interest on its own.

We talked about her other smaller assets, her car, some silver, a bit of jewellery. I asked, *"What else? What have you excluded?"*

She paused. She did not know. So I mentioned her substantial superannuation. *"Oh yes!"* she laughed. *"I forgot about that."*

Then we looked at her future inheritance. And her future earnings.

In that moment, she realised she could easily be a millionaire, or greater, well before any so-called "retirement."

It was an exciting moment for both of us. Nothing new had been added, she simply saw what was already there. From that awareness, a different choice could be made.

Try This

Take a quiet hour. Pull out a blank sheet of paper.

Write down everything you own, the obvious and the hidden.
Add in the "less obvious":

- Superannuation, 401K.
- Insurance payouts you are entitled to.
- Possible inheritance.
- Items of value you have forgotten.
- Skills, knowledge, connections that generate value when you choose to use them.

Look at that list and ask:

If I include all of this, what new choices open up for me?

No More Pretending

Nothing here is right or wrong, it is simply about including it. When you acknowledge what you have, you give yourself a bigger base to create from.

You are not starting from lack. You are starting from wealth, and choosing what else you would like to add.

Next up

Let's look at what it means to trust *you*, and trust your awareness more than anyone else's advice about money.

Awareness, Trusting You Above All Else

We live in an age of noise, and everywhere you turn, there is an expert telling you what to do with your money.

There are studies, podcasts, influencers, headlines, and predictions, all very certain, all very convincing, all often contradicting each other.

The more information there is, the harder it can be to hear the simplest voice: your own.

Awareness is Now

Awareness is not a rule book. It is not someone else's system. It is not a forecast or a promise.

Awareness is what you know right now. It is the tiny shift in your gut that says, *"This works for me,"* or *"This does not."* It is the quiet clarity underneath the mental chatter.

A Small Example

You might read an article about the "best investment." The charts look solid, the graphs point up. The author sounds confident. But when you sit quietly and ask, *"Will this work for me?"* you feel a wobble in your stomach. Or a little sense of *not now.*

That is awareness.

Gut Knowing vs. Mind Noise

It is tempting to call this "trust your gut," and that is partly true. But sometimes your gut is full of old beliefs too. The real tool is you, the being, choosing to trust what you know beyond the mind's panic or the gut's old reactions.

The simplest question I use all the time, *Will this work for me?*

Not, *Will this work for them?* Not, *Does this sound good?*
Will this work for me, here, now, with what I know?

Experts are Not Wrong, They are Not You

Experts can be brilliant. They offer useful tools, ideas, perspectives. They may even point you to possibilities you had not considered yet. That is great.

But they cannot choose for you. They cannot sense what is light or heavy in your world. They do not live your life.

When you trust you, you become the greatest asset you have. You can receive the input, weigh it, and ask, *Does this match what I know is possible?* If yes, use it. If not, thank it and walk on.

A Simple Practice

Next time you are about to make a money choice, big or small, pause. Ask:

Is this true for me?
Will this work for me?
If I choose this, what will my future be like, and if I do not choose this what will my future be like?

You may not get a perfect "answer." You may just feel lighter, or heavier. Trust that sense, it is you.

There is Only You

You can look everywhere for answers. Or you can know you have the clearest one inside you, always.

No one else knows what is true for you. Only you do.

When you trust that, wealth gets lighter, choices get clearer, and life opens wider than any expert could predict.

Next up

Let's look at the old structures so many people still live by, and how to choose beyond what was created for a world that no longer exists.

You can't have money when you're committed to staying indebted to your future.

What Was Created Then Does Not Work Now

So much of what people struggle with today was never really theirs.

It was created by people who came before, in times that looked nothing like now.

Retirement, for example. The "gold watch" age. Forty years in one job, one company, a house you pay off in thirty years, then slow down and fade out. That model made sense when it was designed. For its time, it was perfect.

But is that time still here?

The Structures of Then

So many structures are still running, long after the world moved on:

- The idea that work must be hard to be valuable.
- That you should buy a house, get a loan, pay it off, repeat.
- That you must retire at 65, whether you want to or not.
- That you should "budget down" instead of create more.

They all made sense once, for people who needed certainty, stability, a single job for life.

But are they true for you now?

Perfect For Its Time

My father bought things that were brilliant for his time. My mother kept habits that were needed for her time. Some of those habits were passed to me, as they were to you.

And that is fine. Those habits and actions got us here. But the trouble comes when we live inside structures that no longer match the world, or the lives we would like to create.

Living in a New Time

Look around. Do you see people still operating like it is 1975? Like it is 1995? Or even 2005?

They use the same money rules, the same career rules, the same spending habits. They stay in jobs they do not enjoy because it is "the way." They keep debt alive because it feels normal. They retire not because they want to, but because the system says so.

None of it is wrong. But does it work now? Does it create more for you, or keep you repeating someone else's idea of a life?

You Do Not Have to Break It, Just Choose

You do not have to protest, burn it down, or fix the whole system.
You can simply choose beyond it.

You can look at every rule you inherited, about work, money, wealth, debt, saving, spending, and ask, *Does this actually work for me? Or was it perfect for then, and not now?*

When you see it clearly, you get your choice back.

Try This

Look at one habit you learned about money or work from your parents, teachers, or culture.

Ask, *Was this created for a different time?*
And, *If I did not have to follow this structure anymore, what could I choose instead?*

What more could be possible?

Everything you have read so far invites this same question, *What more could be possible for you, right now?*

You can honour what came before, and still choose what works for you now.

That is freedom.

Next up

Let's look at how the cost-of-living pushes people to shrink their life, and how you can choose to create more instead.

The Cost of Living, Shrink it or Create More

O ne thing you will hear a lot these days is: *"The cost of living is up, you have to cut back."*

Cut back on coffees. Cut back on dinners out. Cut back on wine, holidays, takeaways, nice shoes, the good petrol. Shrink, shrink, shrink.

And sometimes that works, for a while. Until you realise you are living a smaller life to fit inside a number you decided you cannot expand.

The Usual Reaction

I caught myself doing this at the petrol station. I would pull up and look at the price signs for 91, 95, 98 (octane). I would buy the cheapest, even though my car ran better on the good stuff.

It saved a few dollars. But over time, it cost more, lowered performance, increased the cost of maintenance and created more worry about what I was "spending."

One day I asked myself, *What would it take for the price of fuel to never matter again?*
What if instead of shrinking my life to fit a number, I chose to create more money, so the number stopped being a limit?

Is Budgeting Bad?

Budgeting is not wrong. It can be smart, simple and satisfying. Some people love it, they find freedom in clear lines and known limits. That is a valid choice.

But budgeting should not become a cage. If you use it to squeeze life smaller and smaller, you will eventually notice you are budgeting the joy out of your days.

What if you did not have to shrink your life, or stretch it to breaking point?

What if you simply asked, *How much more can I create?*

A Small Example

I knew someone who would spend hours hunting for second-hand bargains online, just to save $100 on something new.

They would drive across town, meet strangers, haggle, wait, reschedule, get frustrated. By the time they got home, they had spent half a day for a tiny saving.

What they did not see was the hidden cost, **their own time.**

Your time has value, real value. But most people spend it like it is free. They will trade hours to save dollars, forgetting that those hours could be used to create more money, more freedom, or more of the life they say they are shrinking expenses to afford.

What is your time really worth? And do you ever include that when you chase a "bargain"?

The question is not simply, *How can I spend less?*

The real question is, *How can I use my time to create more?*

Choice: Shrink or Expand

Your life costs something to run, that is not going away. But the shape of your life is yours to choose.

You can shrink it down to fit your current income, or you can choose to create more income so the life you would love can grow bigger than any price rise.

There is no right or wrong, just a question of what feels lighter for you.

Try This

Next time you catch yourself saying, *"I can't afford that,"* pause.

Ask, *What would it take to create enough money that this is not a question?*
Or, *What else could I add to my life that brings in more revenue, instead of cutting it back?*

What More Could Be Possible for You, Right Now?

What if the cost of living was never the thing that shrank your life, but the thing that invited you to create more, live larger, and keep choosing possibility?

Next up

Let's wrap all these threads into a fresh look at *True Financial Freedom*, the kind that is never about the number alone.

How much of your life are you
spending trying to prove you're good
with money, instead of having it?

True Financial Freedom, it Was Never About the Money Alone

P eople talk about financial freedom like it is a number.

A million in the bank.
No debt.
Passive income streams.
A retirement fund big enough to never run out.

And all those things can be wonderful, if you choose them. But they are not freedom by themselves.

What is Freedom, Really?

Real financial freedom is not about a fixed dollar amount. It is about the *space* to choose.

It is about knowing you can create money when you choose to.
It is about knowing you can receive it, have it, keep it, without fear that you will lose it or sabotage it.
It is about being present with your life, the costs, the assets, the flow, and choosing what you would like to change or expand, moment by moment.

It is about the trust that no matter what happens, market shifts, unexpected bills, new adventures, you are the source, not the victim.

Freedom is a Choice

Freedom is not a point you arrive at. It is a way you travel.

If you make "enough money" the goal, you might hit it, then shrink your life to keep it safe, or lose it and feel like you have failed.

But if you make choice the way you create, you can have more than any single target. You are never finished. You are never stuck. You always have another arrow to fire.

The Money Was Never the Point

All the stories in this book, about debt, spending, having, targets, trust, point to one simple truth:

Money is not the difficulty.
Money is not the limit.
Money is not the freedom.

You are.

An Invitation

So here, at the "end," is the only real question:

What future would you like to choose now?

And, *What more could be possible for you, right now?*

You choose.
You always did.

Reflections to Take With You

T his book was never about giving you the "right" way to do money.

It is an invitation to notice what you had not seen before, and to choose from there.

Below are some of the questions, ideas, and awarenesses you have met along the way. You do not have to remember them all. But if one speaks to you now, take it with you.

Spending vs. Having

Are you spending to get rid of money, or choosing to have it?
One creates flow. The other maintains lack.

Debt as a Commitment to the Past

Debt often is not about the purchase, it is about what you have committed your future to.
Are you choosing freedom, or sustaining the story that you cannot have money?

Knowing What Your Life Costs

Clarity is not control. It is freedom.
When you know what your life costs to run, you can create more, instead of shrinking your choices.

Targets, Not Goals

Goals are fixed. Targets move.
With targets, you can always shoot again, and you do not fail just because you missed one.

Choice Creates

What if you did not wait until the money showed up?

What if you chose first, and let the Universe get to work?

Receiving More Than Money

Many people think their problem is with money.
Often, it is a difficulty with receiving.
Are you willing to receive money, kindness, help, ease and fun, or are you only willing to work for it?

Your Awareness is Your Wealth

The more present you are with money, the more you can have of it.
No shame. No story. Just awareness.

You are the Source

Financial freedom is not a number.
It is the awareness that you can choose again, create more, and trust yourself to handle anything.

What Comes Next?

You do not need more answers. You already know.
Sometimes it is quiet. Sometimes it is inconvenient.
But you know.
If this book gave you something, a shift, a breath, a question, we invite you to follow that.

Stay connected. Watch for what we create next.

And if you would like to go further with these ideas in a hands-on, real-time way... there's more coming.

Thank you for reading. Thank you for choosing.

You are not wrong. You never were.

—Simone & Stephen

About the Authors

Stephen Outram has enjoyed careers and business in architecture, illustration, CGI, graphic design, and with a Master of Science Degree, 20+ years in IT. He is a multibook author spanning fiction and nonfiction, all exploring what lies beneath the obvious, in money, work, living, and the hidden choices people make. Stephen invites people to become aware of the living choices they have available, often hidden from view.

Simone Phillips is an experienced senior and deeply respected schoolteacher, known for her warm presence, clear perspective, and the unique way she encourages others to care for themselves while caring for the world. She is the author of *From*

Carergiver to Caring and has contributed to several books as translator, editor and story contributor. Her passion lies in education, language acquisition and behaviour management, and she teaches business and economics. She has spoken at conferences presenting contemporary strategies and activities that bring liveliness to language classrooms.

Stay Connected

M any of the ideas in this book were born in real time, in the unscripted conversations we share on our YouTube channel, Mouth Buzz.

Mouth Buzz

This is where we talk about life, money, choices, awareness, and everything in between. Sometimes it is deep, sometimes it is light, and it is always alive, just like the pages you have read here.

If you would like to keep playing with these ideas, join us here:

- mouthbuzz.com (points directly to our channel)

- or find us on YouTube:
  youtube.com/@mouthbuzz
- and other popular social platforms.

Subscribe to our channels, mailing list and keep in touch with new releases or events we may be speaking at.

Thank you for reading and for choosing more.

—Simone & Stephen

Stephen Outram & Simone Phillips

Your Notes

Why Saving Can Send You Broke

Stephen Outram & Simone Phillips

www.ingramcontent.com/pod-product-compliance
Lightning Source LLC
Chambersburg PA
CBHW060139050426
42448CB00010B/2208